ROTHENBURG
AND THE
TAUBER VALLEY

Dear Guest,

We hope you enjoy our selection of itinerary-related books. This book is part of our ship library and you are more than welcome to take it to your stateroom. Please return when you are finished so that other guests may also enjoy it.

Thank you for your cooperation,
Your Hotel Manager

Text by
Ralf Nestmeyer

Photos by
Ulrike Romeis
and Josef Bieker

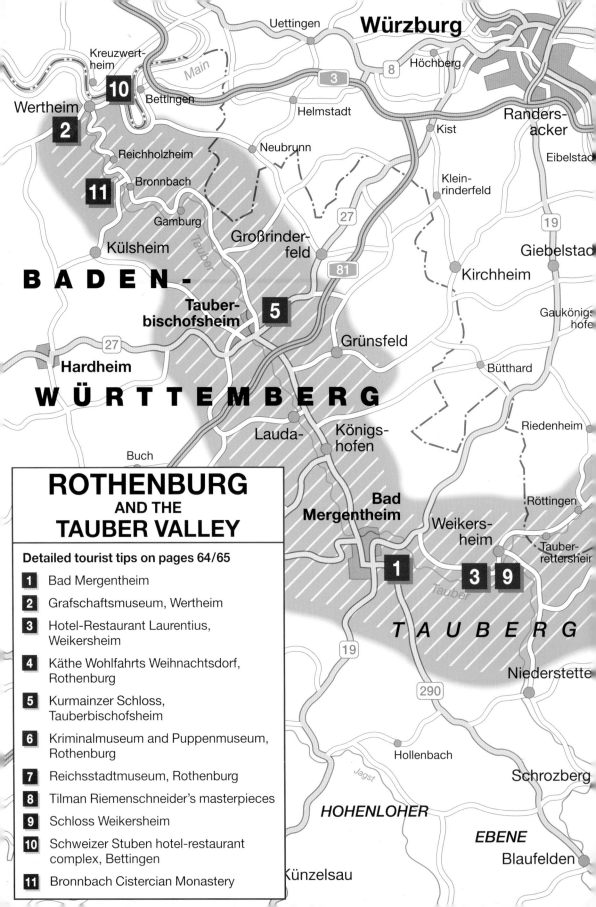

Uettingen

Würzburg

Kreuzwert-
heim

Main

Höchberg

8

3

Randers-
acker

10

Bettingen

Helmstadt

Kist

Wertheim

Eibelstad

2

Neubrunn

Reichholzheim

Klein-
rinderfeld

Bronnbach

11

27

Giebelstad

19

Gamburg

Kirchheim

Külsheim

Großrinder-
feld

BADEN-

81

Gaukönig
hofe

Tauber-
bischofsheim

5

Grünsfeld

Bütthard

Hardheim

WÜRTTEMBERG

Riedenheim

Lauda-

Königs-
hofen

Röttingen

Buch

ROTHENBURG
AND THE
TAUBER VALLEY

**Bad
Mergentheim**

Weikers-
heim

Tauber-
rettersheir

1

3

9

Detailed tourist tips on pages 64/65

T A U B E R G

Niederstette

19

290

Hollenbach

Schrozberg

HOHENLOHER

Jagst

EBENE

Künzelsau

Blaufelden

Stürtz REGIO

ROTHENBURG
AND THE
TAUBER VALLEY

Text by
Ralf Nestmeyer

Photos by
Ulrike Romeis
and Josef Bieker

The Authors:

Ralf Nestmeyer studied history and philosophy. He lives and works in Nuremberg as a freelance travel and culture journalist. He also writes for various newspapers and is the author of numerous travel guides.

Ulrike Romeis is a freelance photographer in Dortmund. She has received many awards and art prizes for her photographic work.

Josef Bieker is a freelance photographer in Dortmund. His work has been published in a great number of travel journals and books.

Credits

Photos:
Archiv für Kunst und Geschichte, Berlin: p. 42 bottom.

Sigloch Bildarchiv, Künzelsau: p. 58.

Käthe Wohlfahrt Archives: p. 36 left and right.

Stürtz Verlag archives: p. 25 top, p. 32 top and bottom, p. 33 left, p. 50 top right and bottom left.

Die Deutsche Bibliothek – CIP catalogue record
Rothenburg and the Tauber Valley / Ulrike Romeis and Josef Bieker (photographers)
Ralf Nestmeyer (author).–
Würzburg: Stürtz 1998.
ISBN 3–8003–1122–4 / paperback

Design: Förster Illustration & Grafik, Rimpar
Cartography: Steffen Oberländer, Munich
Repro: Atelier Hofmüller, Linz
Translation: Ruth Chitty, Schweppenhausen
Printed and edited by the
Universitätsdruckerei H. Stürtz AG, Würzburg

ISBN 3–8003–1122–4 / paperback

CONTENTS

THE "PRETTIEST TRIBUTARY OF THE MAIN"

The Weißer Turm at the end of Georgengasse. Built onto it is the former Judentanzhaus, the intellectual centre of Rothenburg's Jewish community in the Middle Ages.

Not by chance is Rothenburg ob der Tauber considered the ideal of a romantic town. Protected by strong walls and mighty towers, riddled with narrow streets and old half-timbered houses, the venerable free city of the Holy Roman Empire stretches elegantly along a ridge above the Tauber Valley, the St. Jakobskirche with its raised choir and unequal spires rising majestically above the steep roofs. Rothenburg is at its most impressive in the afternoon or early evening, when – coming from the west –

the town's striking silhouette glistens in the sun,

View of the town walls, a symbol of power and glory from the time when Rothenburg was a free city of the Holy Roman Empire. To the right is the imposing Faulturm.

more beautiful than any film or theatre backdrop. The unique symbiosis of town and countryside is unparalleled in Germany and draws visitors like a magnet, however sentimental or emotionally sober their disposition.

Most come here primed on the illusion of an untouched medieval world which they hope to find in the winding streets and painted timbers. Mentally armed with Romantic literature, fed on verses by Eichendorff and Mörike, Ludwig Richter illustrations before their eyes, Rothenburg is their nostalgic dream come true. Artisans, antique dealers and a flourishing souvenir trade ensure that long after the visit this professed love for the traditional lives on in the various abodes of Rothenburg's bevy of tourists.

Those who prefer empty streets and quiet corners would be best advised to visit Rothenburg at dead of night. By day the town is overrun by visitors from all over the world. Around two-and-a-half million guests are counted each year. Critics see Rothenburg as conserved idyll, a kind of medieval Disneyland, and are keen to point out that shortly before the end of the Second World War over a third of the town was reduced to ruins during an American air raid and that the old part of town between the Weißer Turm and Rödertor is actually nothing more

mous range and number of artistic treasures here. A walk along or around the town walls – almost two miles of them – with 43 gateways and defensive towers gives you an excellent impression of

the former greatness of this once fearless city.

Its beginnings were modest; towards the end of the 10th century the Counts of Kochergau chose a narrow ridge above the Tauber River as a good, defensive place to build their castle, in whose shadow a small

The Röderbogen, with its roof turret set at a slight angle, was built in the 16th century to replace an earlier town gate.

than an exact reconstruction of the original. All that glitters is not gold…

Despite this, Rothenburg lives with – and off – its past. You need plenty of time to fully appreciate the enor-

market settlement arose – the nucleus of modern-day Rothenburg.

There's not much left of the Counts' castle, but the view from the castle gardens of Taubergrund is magnificent. From here you can also see

You can still walk along nearly all of the covered wall walks in the Spitalviertel (right) and along Klingenschütt (bottom right). The Klingentorturm, almost 100 feet high, used to be a water tower.

Heinrich Toppler had a tower house built in 1388 (above) to guard the 24 water mills in Taubergrund. It also served him as a prestigious holiday home.

the rather lonely, fairy-tale Topplerschlösschen, a tower house built by Rothenburg's most eminent mayor, Heinrich Toppler, wanting to leave a memorial to himself. His wish was fully justified, for under his skilled administration Rothenburg reached the pinnacle of its powerful career.

In around 1400 more than 6,000 people dwelled within the mighty city walls.

The city state's lands spread out over approximately 150 square miles and included 167 villages and several castles. Toppler represented the affairs of the free city with impressive confidence before the nobles of the empire and wasn't afraid to mount his war-horse when he had to. For the outside world, Toppler was Rothenburg incarnate. Yet it is common knowledge that those who wield power make enemies. When Toppler overexerted his drive for diplomatic supremacy to the detriment of the city, he met with a sorry end. The city councillors had him arrested and following a very dubious trial Toppler was executed on June 13, 1408, in the dungeons under the town hall.

Rothenburg's splendour as a free city was destined not to last much longer. During the Thirty Years' War the town sided with the Protestant Union and was taken twice by the opposing forces. The town's spirit was broken with lasting effects on city economy and politics. A good century later the citizens' defensive *élan* had waned so much as to be tantamount to almost nothing; during the Seven Years' War it took a mere 35 hussars under one lieutenant to seize Rothenburg and pillage it. And in 1802, the year Rothenburg fell to Bavaria, independence as a free city finally became a thing of the past.

Artists such as Ludwig Richter and Carl Spitzweg,

on their quest for Biedermeier charm, began wandering through town with their pencils, brushes and sketch books; a few years later travellers made curious about Rothenburg's cultural offerings through reports in the paper positively stormed the city gates. The good burghers of Rothenburg were quick to realise the tourist potential of their picturesque home. They wanted to "offer travellers everything to make their stay in Rothenburg as pleasant as possible". This wasn't

Episodes from the town's past are depicted in the historic vaults under the town hall.

Herrngasse was a popular address with Rothenburg's old-established patrician families. Staudt'scher Hof demonstrates how they lived. Here (bottom right) the kitchen is shown.

Not graced by the benedictions of the modern industrial age, Rothenburg sank into a deep sleep. It didn't awake from its medieval daze until it was discovered by 19th-century tourism as the romantic metropolis of Germany.

limited to the sudden abundance of rooms proffered for rent by esteemed craftsmen; the whole town was transformed into a neat little tourist attraction, the piles of dung banished to outside the city gates and the city's glorious history celebrated

The external trademarks of Franconia's inns are their wrought-iron pub signs. The town's well-known Glocke, Eisenhut and Riemenschneider hotels honour the tradition.

in lavish plays and legends about Heinrich Toppler and the drinking skills of senior town mayor Georg Nusch. Their efforts were rewarded with success; today people all over the world think of

Rothenburg ob der Tauber as the "gingerbread house of the German soul".

It was also in Rothenburg that Wilhelm Heinrich Riehl began his famous walk which led to him being heralded the "discoverer" of the Tauber Valley. In a travel report he later published in Augsburg's *Allgemeine Zeitung* the well-known folklorist and art historian described the towns and villages in the Tauber Valley, coining the much-quoted phrase: "A journey through the Tauber Valley is a journey through German history, a modern journey through the old empire." In autumn 1865 Riehl hiked from Rothenburg to Wertheim and in those few miles he found places

which had held on to their Franconian traditions despite Napoleonic changes to the region. For at the beginning of the 19th century the self-appointed French emperor put an end to Germany's huge

Old handicrafts, almost forgotten in our modern age, are revived during the Reichsstadt Festtage in September. Here, wickerwork.

number of small states once and for all, dividing the patchwork territory of the Tauber Valley into three and distributing it to the states Bavaria, Baden and Württemberg, all members of the Confederation of the Rhine. In doing so he completely disregarded any historical bonds between the Tauber communities, linked by local dialect, architecture and custom. Needless to say, this was an unpopular move on Napoleon's part. In Mergentheim early in the summer of 1809 the peasants armed themselves and rebelled

The inhabitants of the Tauber Valley claim that their valley is full of beauty and charm –

and this is absolutely true. Between Rothenburg and Wertheim, where after an 80-mile journey the Tauber flows into the Main, the river meanders through lovely countryside draped in vineyards and peppered with ancient towns and churches, making a trip through the valley

Half-timbered houses on Rödergasse, a sign of former prosperity, with the Röderbrunnen in the foreground.

against their new lord, the king of Württemberg. Only after many peasants had lost their lives in a battle at Wartberg could the revolt be crushed by the king. Grudges were long born; even as late as in 1973 the citizens of Wertheim deliberately snubbed their state government (Baden–Württemberg) by flying the Bavarian flag. And Würzburg is still closer to the hearts of people in the Tauber Valley than Munich or Stuttgart.

well worth it for cyclists and art lovers in particular. The Herrgottskirche not far from Creglingen, for example, houses a remarkable gem in the form of Tilman Riemenschneider's Altar of the Assumption. Weikersheim, the ancestral seat of the Hohenlohe dynasty, is dominated by a splendid Renaissance castle with Baroque gardens and an orangery, and the opulent palace of the Teutonic Order towers above royal residence Bad Mergentheim,

The splendid Gelbes Haus on Karlsberg near Weikersheim used to be part of a palatial hunting lodge belonging to the Hohenlohe family. It is now a restaurant (below).

Schloss Weikersheim (above right) more than adequately illustrates the cravings of the past age for prestige. The decorative gables were added at the end of the 16th century. The gardens are Baroque.

Eduard von Mörike lived on Bad Mergentheim's Marktplatz from 1844–1851 (bottom right).

where three major holiday routes converge (the Romantische Straße, the Schwäbische Weinstraße and the Dichterstraße).

"There is a little town in Taubergrund which I constantly laud and praise, where life is so fine",

wrote poet Eduard Mörike, who enjoyed early retirement in Mergentheim from 1844 to 1851. Mörike also enthused about the healing properties of Wilhelmsquelle spring water, discovered a few years previously by a shepherd, enough so to pen a fitting verse: "Those tired of life / or indisposed / can be helped, / God be praised, / If they care to take / the waters of / Mergentheim's healing springs." In 1926 Mergentheim was granted permission to put "Bad" before its name, bestowing upon it the cher-

ished status of spa. Today four different mineral springs ease the ailments of those suffering from disorders of the digestive system, liver or gall bladder.

Further north lies Tauberbischofsheim, world-famous for its fencing and administrative capital of the

Main-Tauber district. Its historical architectural make-up has unfortunately suffered great loss, but the area between the Kurmainzer Schloss and the market place still has a tranquil flair to it. The little town of Niklashausen also appears quite leisurely, but this wasn't always the case. A relief in the village church recalls Hans Böhm, better known locally as the "piper of Niklashausen". A socio-revolutionary preacher, he rebelled against the ruling princes and bishops and was burnt at the stake as a heretic in Würzburg in 1476. A little way further down the Tauber in Bronnbach the imposing monastery buildings, affiliated to the famous Cistercian monastery at Maulbronn, take up the entire breadth of the valley. The austere architecture, built according to guidelines set by the leading figure of the order, Bernhard of Clairvaux, still breathes the spirit of the Cistercian monks.

The final highlight of the valley tour is Wertheim, a pretty riverside town

with lots of half-timbered houses. From the vast castle ruins there is a wonderful view of the Tauber, of the "prettiest tributary of the Main" as it has often been called. ■

Ruined Burg Wertheim. The former home to the Counts of Wertheim is one of the largest castles in Germany. It was destroyed in the Thirty Years' War.

*Previous double
spread: from the top
of the Röderturm
only the town hall
and Jakobskirche
transcend the
sea of roofs in
Old Rothenburg.*

The houses in Rothenburg's old town, such as here in the Spitalviertel (main photo), are often squashed up against the town walls. Gerlachschmiede near the Rödertor with its steep gable (bottom right) and the huge Hegereiterhaus (bottom left), where once the administrators of the spital's lands resided, are no exception.

From the Rödertor with its bastion and the two toll and guard houses (top right) you pass under the Röderbogen (centre right) to the town hall.

Following double spread: Plönlein, a small square in front of the Siebersturm, is the most-photographed and most-painted corner of Rothenburg.

21

THE MIDDLE AGES REVISITED

Re-enacting life in camp as a medieval guild is part and parcel of the Reichsstadt Festtage.

Town life in Rothenburg reaches a colourful climax in the Reichsstadt Festtage which take place in September each year. They were initiated in 1974 to commemorate the 700th anniversary of Rothenburg being made a free city of the Holy Roman Empire. During the three days of the festival, the old town is transformed into

one huge, frenetic open-air stage.

The festival is opened with an atmospheric torchlight procession of all the participating historical

No music, no festival: drumming up a storm in the narrow streets, night-time concerts in the squares.

groups through the expectant streets of Rothenburg on Friday evening. Over the weekend, visitors milling through the streets and squares can witness the major events in the city's history. Dressed in authentic costume, amateur actors are

charitable Franciscan monks, rebellious peasants armed with scythes and flails, medieval minstrels and bold knights – or judges at mock trials who mete out suitable punishments to wrongdoers. On Saturday evening the town is bombarded by canons and fire in memory of the Thirty Years' War – all a pyrotechnic illusion, of course. The festival programme also wouldn't be complete without performances of the historic Shepherd's Dance and the *Meistertrunk* saga, famous far beyond the city boundaries.

The man credited with the authorship of the *Meistertrunk* legend is Rothenburg chronicler Heinrich Schaffert (1739–1794). There is no historical proof of the episode from the Thirty Years' War on which local poet Adam Hörber based his play, first performed in 1881 in Rothenburg. The story goes that Field Marshal Tilly was so incensed at Rothenburg's resistance during the war that in autumn 1631 he planned to torch the city and have the councillors executed. Yet when he was handed Rothenburg's welcome drink, a tankard holding over half a gallon of wine, he promised the burghers that if one of them had the

"strength and courage to empty the tankard in one draught",

he would show mercy. Senior mayor Nusch stepped forward and demonstrated his incredible powers of consumption, which left Tilly so impressed that he took back his violent threats and spared the city.

The audience at the premiere of the drama was so enthusiastic that the *Meistertrunk* legend was granted not only a permanent place in the municipal festival calendar but soon materialised as a clock decorating the gable of the Ratstrinkstube.

Now, when the clock strikes the hour, burgomaster Nusch appears at his clock window and dutifully drains his tankard, while in the opposite window Field Marshal Tilly signals his admiration with a wave of his baton. ■

Rothenburg honours its Meistertrunk saga, where senior mayor Nusch is said to have saved his town from destruction during the Thirty Years' War, in a number of ways. There's a Meistertrunk play, works of art and even a clock adorning the gable of the Ratstrinkstube on the market place. Field Marshal Tilly and burgomaster Nusch have appeared on the hour between 11 a.m. and 3 p.m. and 8 p.m. and 10 p.m. every day since 1910 (below).

A mere stone's throw from the Stein- and Herren- mühle (above) is the mighty twin bridge over the Tauber, one of the most impressive monuments to medieval engineering in Germany.

Rothenburg positively towers above Taubergrund down in the river valley. You can enter the town from the famous twin bridge via the Kobolzeller Tor (top). The steep climb is well rewarded by excellent views of the Tauber riviera.

Rothenburg's castle was destroyed during an earthquake in 1356; the grounds have been turned into a pleasure garden. From here you have wonderful views of the Spitalviertel.

Six gates once guarded access to Rothenburg. As opposed to the rather insignificant Burgtor (top right), Klingentor is highly defensive with its weighty bastion.

Following double spread: Marktplatz is only this empty during the small hours. By day the market place is the bustling heart of town. It is dominated by the wonderful Renaissance façade of the town hall with its corner oriel, stair tower and Baroque arcades. The gable tower of the rear, Gothic part of the complex is almost 200 feet high. To the right is the Ratstrinkstube.

DREAMING OF A BETTER WORLD

Rothenburg ob der Tauber is seen as the epitome of German Romanticism among Germany's old cities. With its Gothic churches, fortified walls and towers, narrow, crooked streets and well-restored half-timbered houses,

Rothenburg stirs up longing for the days of yore.

A longing for the past, for the (idealised) Middle Ages of knights in shining armour, travelling merchants and pious monks which also gripped those poets who established Romanticism's literary movement, such as Wackenroder, Tieck, Novalis, Eichendorff and Brentano. This was the rebellion of the subjectivity of the mind and the soul against the Enlightenment and its doctrine of rationalism and utility, which denied life all that was poetic.

Typical Rothenburg scenes captured by the Romantics: Ludwig Richter's Der Wacholderbaum (above) and Carl Spitzweg's Der Institutsspaziergang (c. 1860, below) and Der Abschied (c. 1855, p. 33).

Not one of the great Romantics actually ever visited Rothenburg. It was lesser-known Romantic artist Ludwig Richter who, on a hiking tour in 1826, came across the little town on the Tauber and was moved enough to record the following in his memoirs: "The houses with their tall, pointed gables, each floor jutting out over the one below, antiquated signs

and guild marks, Gothic chapels and churches, yet few people on the streets and in the alleys: everything was so quiet in this twilight!

I felt as if I had been whisked back to the Middle Ages,

especially when I entered the inn. [I opened] a small Gothic door, went down two steps into the hallway. The lounge had a low ceiling and small windows with round panes. A few men were seated at the tables dressed in garments their grandfathers may have worn, their beer in tall, tin tankards I know of only from Albrecht Dürer."

"a little Gothic Swabian place encircled by defensive walls and full of ancient architectural gems". In the years to come artists Richter and Spitzweg were followed by hundreds of travellers overjoyed at the cobbled streets of Rothenburg; time and again the Tauber metropolis stilled the unfulfilled yearning for a (supposedly) intact world long gone. The word "romantic" is still the predominant feature of adverts and marketing ploys intent on enticing potential visitors. No surprise, then, that the "Romantic Route" (Romantische Straße), invented in 1950, passes through the "charming Tauber Valley" and Rothenburg before meandering off to Dinkelsbühl,

The Reichsstadt Festtage on Plönlein also honour the artists of the Romantic period who discovered the beauty of Rothenburg (then totally unheard of) in the 19th century.

In the wake of Romanticism trotted the petit-bourgeois world of the Biedermeier period. Looking for motifs for his provincial interior paintings, none other than artist Carl Spitzweg came to the Tauber Valley in 1858 where he found

Nördlingen and Donauwörth. All are old towns in an excellent state of preservation who experienced their cultural and political high point in the Late Middle Ages – the era so celebrated by the Romantics. ■

You have marvellous
views of Rothenburg
from atop the tower
of the town hall.
From here you notice
how narrow the
houses often are,
their gables always
facing streetwards,
such as here on
the market place
(bottom right).

The statue on the
ornate St. Georgs
Brunnen from 1608
on Marktplatz depicts
St. George engaged
in combat with the
famous dragon.
To the left is the oriel
of Jagstheimerhaus
with a reverent
madonna.

The notable
Baumeisterhaus on
Obere Schmiedgasse
(above left and right)
has a resplendent,
lavishly decorated
sandstone façade
and a secluded, leafy
courtyard for a romantic
rendezvous with
the past.

365 DAYS OF CHRISTMAS

A huge nutcracker soldier stands guard at 1, Herrngasse, in Rothenburg. Those brave enough to slip past him into the building probably think Christmas is celebrated 365 days of the year in the Tauber city.

of Rothenburg's sights and attractions. For numerous foreign visitors, whether from Atlanta, Tokyo or Gelsenkirchen, Christmas shopping is just as important an item on the agenda as exploring the medieval walls.

May all your dreams come true at Käthe Wohlfahrt's Weihnachtsdorf – even if you're too old to believe in Father Christmas.

Memories of long-lost childhoods are refreshed in Käthe Wohlfahrt's sprawling Christmas Village (Weihnachtsdorf). The Christmas bazaar with its labyrinth of aisles and shelves is a winter wonderland; over 13,000 feet of tinsel, 80,000 Christmas tree lights and pounds and pounds of plastic snow create a unique atmosphere which easily puts the Käthe Wohlfahrt Weihnachtsdorf on a par with the rest

Company founder Wilhelm Wohlfahrt didn't dare dream that his shop would become such a huge triumph. Rothenburg's many other businessmen and women were also more than sceptical. When Wohlfahrt started setting up the first all-year Christmas store (Christkindlmarkt) in Europe in 1977 future fellow traders shook their heads in amazement, as if Wohlfahrt was going to try to

Käthe Wohlfahrt

sell beach fashion in the middle of winter. Shop assistants were hard to find; nobody wanted to take on such an unsteady job. Yet Wohlfahrt's concept caught on. Demand for high-quality Christmas decor proved to be far from sat-

isfied – and as hoped didn't let up in the summer months. Wohlfahrt's ambitious idea was a roaring success.

Even before the planned inauguration there were so many noses being pressed against the glass in anticipation, demanding to be let in, that without further ado the grand opening of the Christkindlmarkt was put forward a day. Four

years later, on the opposite side of the street, Wohlfahrt flung open the doors to his now

world-famous Weihnachtsdorf,

whose centrepiece is an impressive, 18-foot white Christmas tree. It positively sparkles with its 7,240 fairy lights and 1,000 baubles.

Regardless of what has taken their particular fancy – coloured glass baubles, decorations made of tin or wood from the Erzgebirge, gold foil angels, typical German nutcrackers

or pipe-smokers, music boxes or crib figures – fans of traditional German Christmas feel as if they're in paradise in the attractively decorated premises. There's everything from hand-painted filigree miniatures in limited editions to designer decorations produced by the Wohlfahrt business itself, available in all tones and hues to coordinate with the purchaser's home decor 365 days a year. ▨

Shopping for Christmas decorations at Käthe Wohlfahrt's is a festive experience you won't forget. The wooden figures, glass baubles and gold foil angels are all traditionally made and of extremely high quality, earning them the designation "Kunsthandwerk" (genuine craft).

The people of Rothenburg known how to enjoy themselves: cattle farmers (above) and musicians (bottom left) at the Reichsstadt Festtage sharing a beer and a joke.

The historic Shepherd's Dance on the market place looks back to 1517 when the shepherds' guild was granted the privilege of celebrating once a year in town with music and dance. The colourful event is now staged several times a year.

The monumental high altar (Altar of the Twelve Disciples) in the east choir of the St. Jakobskirche was created in 1466. The figures on the shrine, who include church patron St. Jacob, were fashioned by Hans Multscher and other masters from Ulm. The paintings on the predella and the wings of the altar are by artist Friedrich Herlin from Nördlingen.

Top:
Elisabeth and Jacob
on the Altar of the
Twelve Disciples.
Left: view along
Klingengasse of the
passageway under
the church, with the
Feuerleinserker oriel
in the foreground.
The figure of
St. Louis of Toulouse
is an early work
of Tilman
Riemenschneider's.
It is thought that it
originally decorated
an altar shrine
dedicated to the
saint, the remains
of which are
preserved in the
St. Jakobskirche.

AN ARTISTIC REVOLUTION

Riemenschneider spent four years working on the scene of the Last Supper for his Altar of the Holy Blood (p. 43).
The figure at the centre isn't Jesus, but Judas Iscariot. Right: detail of the left wing relief on the altar: the apostles watching Jesus ride into Jerusalem.

No other artist left as great a mark on Franconian Main art in the Late Middle Ages as Tilman Riemenschneider, known to his contemporaries as the "woodcarver of Würzburg". From the Rhön to the Steigerwald, from Aschaffenburg to Bamberg you can find examples of his epoch-making works of art everywhere, yet if you want to see the Late Gothic altars from Riemenschneider's workshop, the embodiment of perfection, you should travel to the Tauber Valley.

Riemenschneider had the extraordinary talent of breathing life into the wood he worked with,

Tilman Riemenschneider included his own likeness on the Altar of the Assumption in Creglingen (above).

making his figures come alive with his play on light and shadow. Another remarkable feature of his work is the gentle expression of restraint on the faces adorning his altars. Riemenschneider awakens the sympathy of the beholder without having to resort to gold or paint like his peers. His figures tell us the stories of their lives, compel us to suffer with them. The perfect folds in the

figures' clothing and the graceful poise of the hands are further notable characteristics of Riemenschneider's pioneering creativity. In the Tauber Valley it's difficult to decide which of Riemenschneider's famous altars still in existence is artistically the most significant: the Altar of the Holy Blood in Rothenburg's St. Jakobskirche or the Altar of the Assumption in Creglingen, both executed in warm, naturally-aged, honey-coloured limewood? The Altar of the Crucifixion in Detwang, which Riemenschneider originally carved for the

Michaelskapelle in Rothenburg, fades in comparison somewhat as the shrine was later made smaller, spoiling the balance of the composition.

Although the master carried out all his work in the Main region, he wasn't actually a Franconian. Born

Riemenschneider wasn't allowed to grow old gracefully. Master Til sympathised with the rebels during the Peasant War in 1525, a mistake which cost him dearly. Würzburg's prince-bishop tolerated no insurgence in his city and regardless of Riemenschneider's high standing as artist and senior mayor had him

The crucifixion group at the parish church in Aub is one of Riemenschneider's lesser-known works.

in Lower Saxony, Riemenschneider first came to Würzburg while on his travels as a young woodcarver's journeyman. The soft Franconian limewood and the possibilities for expression it offered must have inspired the young man, for a few years later he decided to settle in the diocesan town on the Main and asked the local guild to take him on as an assistant. His incredible talent soon earned him riches, prestige and social advancement which culminated in his being made a councillor and later mayor of Würzburg.

thrown into prison, stripped of his office and possibly even tortured.

And the worst was yet to come; Riemenschneider's incarceration cost him his powers of creativity. The "woodcarver of Würzburg" failed to produce any works of artistic value during the last years of his life. He died in 1531. ■

The major attraction in Detwang (below), a small village in the valley below Rothenburg, is the Kirche St. Peter und Paul (right) with Riemenschneider's Altar of the Crucifixion (bottom right).

The main scene on the shrine of Tilman Riemenschneider's altar at the Herrgottskirche in Creglingen pictures the Assumption of the Blessed Virgin Mary. The novelty of the interpretation is that the disciples are witnesses to the event.

Previous double spread: the bridge at Tauberrettersheim is one of the most beautiful of the Tauber Valley's permanent river crossings.

The lush garden at Schloss Weikersheim with its glorious orangery (top left) effuses a sense of Versailles, on which the residence was modelled. The Gallery of Gnomes (top and bottom right) pays homage to Baroque joie de vivre.

FROM THE HOLY LAND TO THE TAUBER

A cross with a black outline in Bad Mergentheim's municipal coat of arms recalls

the city's former rulers, the Teutonic Knights.

For almost three centuries the Grand and German Masters of the third most powerful military and religious order after the Templars and the Hospitallers resided in this modest little town on the Tauber. But why Mergentheim?

The cross of the Teutonic Order adorned the cloaks and necks of the Teutonic Knights. The order's heralds wore the emblem of the Grand Master (top right).

The Teutonic Order of the Knights of St. Mary's Hospital at Jerusalem was founded in 1190 during the third crusade at the port of Acre on what is now the coast of Israel. It was originally form- ed to tend to the wounded, but only a few years after its founding the members of the order themselves took up arms and joined in the battle for Christianity. After the Holy Land was finally lost

to the Muslims and the crusades abandoned, the order concentrated on extending its lands in East Prussia.

The celibate knights converted the "pagans" in East Prussia with their Bibles and swords and gradually built up a territory of immense proportion. Their greed for land was brought to an abrupt halt only in 1410 when they lost the Battle of Tannenberg against Poland. And when in 1525 Albrecht of Bran- denburg renounced his title of Grand Master and turned the order's Prussian territories into a worldly, Protestant state the order was forced to retreat to its German lands in the Holy Roman Empire. Mer- gentheim was chosen as the new residence of the order's Grand Master.

Mergentheim wasn't selected by chance.

The Teutonic Order had owned plenty of land in and around the Franconian town since 1219, given to it by brothers Henry, Andrew and Frederick of Hohenlohe who were members of the order. Fran- conia was also traditionally home to the majority of the Teutonic Knights and was where the order still had a lot of support despite peasant wars and reforming bodies of thought. The citizens of Mergentheim were less than enthusiastic about the Teutonic Knights' choice of abode, however; they would have preferred to have been given the privileged status of free city instead of having to submit to the totalitarian rule of the German Master.

In 1809 Mergentheim's regal, residential glory was passé.

There was no room for a religious order in Napoleon's new division of Europe.

The Teutonic Order was disbanded and the territories around Mergentheim – despite being Franconian for

The castle of the Teutonic Order in Bad Mergentheim is a colourful mixture of architectural styles. Things to look out for are the Baroque church – partly built according to plans by Balthasar Neumann – and lots of other small details, such as the Renaissance stairs by Blasius Berwart.

The order began building in Mergentheim with great profusion which in time reconciled the inhabitants of Mergentheim to their fate. The medieval moated castle was extended and became a palace offering greater comfort. Bit by bit the town was given a splendid facelift, decorated with Baroque cupolas, chapels, fountains and pictorial pillars.

centuries – were annexed to the new Kingdom of Württemberg. ■

In Lauda, an old wine village
with pretty half-timbered
buildings and a splendid
town gate (top right),
and nearby Gerlachsheim,
famous for its monastic church
(centre right), saints watching
over the bridges ensure safe
passage across the Tauber.

*The town hall
in Grünsfeld from
1580 is graced
with particularly
fine carvings.*

Tucked away in a small side valley of the Tauber, the traditional wine village of Beckstein enjoys a fine, mild climate.

Tauberbischofsheim belonged
to the archbishopric of Mainz
until 1803, as the name of its
palace (Kurmainzer Schloss,
main photo and below) implies.
The 16th-century edifice
is dwarfed by the almost
140 feet of the Türmersturm,
where until into the 19th century
the fire watchman lived.

Above: in a bygone age the inhabitants of Tauberbischofsheim cherished a love for Historicism. Both the parish church (St. Martinskirche) and the town hall on the market place were built in the Neo-Gothic style.

SPELT AND HOME-MADE SAUSAGES

Traditionally, the Tauber Valley is a poor farming region, which is why its pubs and restaurants tend to serve simpler, substantial kinds of meals.

Franconian dishes are predominant for historical reasons,

although a distinct Swabian influence is also detectable in the kitchen in the form of *Maultaschen* or Swabian noodles *(Spätzle),* for example.

In the past common spelt was a much-cultivated grain in the area, so a typical Tauber Franconian meal may start with soup made with unripe spelt. Some restaurants are also a dab hand at delicious spelt burgers. The main dish is usually pork in some form or

The Franconian Main's famous "national dish": Blaue Zipfel.

another, often a roast or a *Schäuferla* fresh from the oven served with home-made dumplings *(Klöße).* Favourite evening snacks are what the locals call *Blaue Zipfel,* small home-made sausages which are cooked and served in a vinegary

stock with onions, leeks, carrots, juniper berries and mustard seed. For those with a sweet tooth, try a Rothenburg snowball *(Schneeball):* short-crust pastry fried in fat which in one variation is then dipped in chocolate.

The Tauber Valley also has a few treats for fish connoisseurs.

Menus offer fresh freshwater fish from the lower reaches of the Tauber, such as Main eel, yet the average *Mittelfranke* prefers carp from home fishing grounds. Carp has to swim three times, so the local saying goes: first in the water, then in melted butter and finally in a light, sweet beer or Franconian wine.

Wine is something the Tauber Valley is particularly good at (and famous for). As long ago as in the

Middle Ages Tauber vintages enjoyed an excellent reputation. Franconian wine is traditionally filled in

Bocksbeutel, wide, rounded bottles with a thin neck which may only be used in certain wine regions. The Glass Museum in Wertheim has a collection of historic *Bocksbeutel,* yet the alleged, proud "birthplace of the *Bocksbeutel*" is not here but Beckstein, a small wine village north of Bad Mergentheim.

Wine was also grown in Rothenburg on the southern bank of the Tauber until 1922, as existing cirque walls and terraces show. The vines have long been replaced by clover, grass and quince trees; the first vineyards are a few miles to the north between Tauberzell and Creglingen. Yet with a bit of luck

vines might once again flourish beneath Rothenburg in a few years' time.

The old-established wine estate Glocke is planning to plant a new vineyard on the Tauber riviera in an attempt to revive Rothenburg's wine-growing tradition. An ambitious undertaking, which, it can only be

hoped, will not be thwarted by too many administrative hurdles... ∎

With a lot of luck vines may once again flourish on the inclines of the Tauber Valley, such as here in Beckstein (top left).

Connoisseurs are more than welcome to try the vintages in the romantic wine cellars at the Glocke estate (centre left). Some of the wooden barrels are lovingly decorated with detailed carvings.

Bronnbach Cistercian Monastery is one of the cultural, historic highlights of the Tauber Valley. The Baroque gardens and the furnishings in the Josephssaal coexist in delightful contrast to the Romanesque buildings, which include the wonderful cloister. The ceiling fresco of the Josephssaal with its stucco surround is the work of Würzburg artist Johann Adam Remele.

Wertheim is at its most attractive seen from the Tauber, with the counts' ruined castle rising up above the collegiate church and the Faulturm. One of the most impressive tombstones in the collegiate church is that of Count John I. It portrays him in full armour with his two wives Margarethe and Uta (top left).

Wertheim has two very interesting churches in the Late Gothic Kilianskapelle (bottom right) and the slightly older collegiate church (Stiftskirche, top right), where for centuries the Counts of Wertheim were laid to rest.

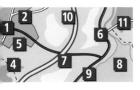

ROTHENBURG AT A GLANCE

This old-timer bus, laden with presents, stands in front of Käthe Wohlfahrt's Christmas Village.

1 Deutschordensmuseum

The main theme of the exhibits in what used to be the **palace of the Teutonic Order** is naturally the **history** of the order itself. The museum also has an extensive **collection of doll's houses.** *(Bad Mergentheim, Schloß 16, tel. +49 (0)79 31/ 5 22 12. Open: Tue – Sun 10 a.m. – 5 p.m.)* If you prefer to experience the great outdoors, stop by **Wildpark Bad Mergentheim** and watch the bears, monkeys and many other wild animals living in Europe's most diverse game park. The **feeding of the wolves** is a thrill not to be missed. *(Bad Mergentheim, tel.+49 (0)79 31/ 4 13 44, fax -4 44 26. Open: Mar – Oct daily 9 a.m. – 7 p.m., Nov – Feb daily 9 a.m. – 6 p.m.)*

A residence fit for the Grand Master of the Teutonic Order in Bad Mergentheim.

2 Grafschaftsmuseum

The county museum has an interesting permanent exhibition on the **history of the county of Wertheim** and an art gallery with many works by **Otto Modersohn.** *(Wertheim, Rathausgasse 10, tel. +49-(0)93 42/30 14 11. Open: Tue – Fri 9.30 a.m. –12 p.m. & 2 – 4 p.m., Sat & Sun 2.30 – 5 p.m.)*

3 Hotel-Restaurant Laurentius

This restaurant on Weikersheim market place offers **top-quality cuisine.** Chef Jürgen Koch is considered one of the most creative cooks in the region. *(Weikersheim, Marktplatz 5, tel. +49-(0)79 34/70 07. Closed Tue)*

Right: local Ochsenfurter Gau costume at the Tauberländer Dorfmuseum.

There are lots of toys for girls and boys at Rothenburg's Puppen- und Spielzeugmuseum (Museum of Dolls and Toys).

4 Käthe Wohlfahrts Weihnachtsdorf

In Europe's largest **all-year Christmas bazaar** fans of German Christmas traditions can find all they need with which to deck the halls for the festive season. *(Rothenburg ob der Tauber, Herrngasse 1, tel. +49-(0)98 61/40 91 50. Open: Mon – Fri 9 a.m. – 6 p.m., Sat 8 a.m. – 4 p.m., mid – May –24 Dec also Sun & public holidays 10 a.m. – 6 p.m.)*

5 Kurmainzer Schloss

The **local museum** in the Kurmainzer Schloss in Tauberbischofsheim has religious art, furniture, traditional peasant dress and also **prehistoric finds.** *(Tauberbischofsheim, tel. +49-(0)93 41/37 60. Open: Easter – 31 Oct Tue – Sat 2.30 – 4.30 p.m., Sun & public holidays 10 a.m. – 12 p.m. & 2.30 – 4.30 p.m.)*

6 Mittelalterliches Kriminalmuseum

The many permanent exhibits of **Germany's major Museum of Crime** offer a fascinating overview of 1,000 years of legal history. Especially the numerous **spectacular instruments of torture** capture the visitors' imagination, among them **scold's bridles** and an **iron maiden.** *(Rothenburg ob der Tauber, Burggasse 3, tel. +49-(0)98 61/53 59. Open: Apr – Oct 9.30 a.m. – 6 p.m. & Nov – Feb 2 – 4 p.m.)* The **Puppen- und Spielzeugmuseum** (Museum of Dolls and Toys) offers a nice contrast to this. *(Hofbronnengasse 13. Open: daily 9 a.m. – 6 p.m.)*

7 Reichsstadtmuseum

Rothenburg's **history as a free city of the Holy Roman Empire** is documented in numerous exhibits, including the valuable **"Rothenburg Passion"** pictorial cycle. *(Rothenburg ob der Tauber, Klosterhof 5, tel. +49-(0)98 61/4 04 58. Open: Mar – Oct 10 a.m. – 5 p.m., Nov – Apr 1 – 4 p.m.)*

8 Riemenschneider

Woodcarver Tilman Riemenschneider's sacral art has left its mark on the Tauber Valley. One of his masterpieces, the **Altar of the Holy Blood,** can be admired in **Rothenburg's St. Jakobskirche.** The **Altar of the Assumption in Creglingen** competes with it for the standing as Riemenschneider's most important piece of work.

9 Schloss Weikersheim

The former residence of the Hohenlohe family began its existence as a moated castle and evolved over the years into a splendid **Renaissance ensemble** with Baroque palace gardens and an orangery. *(Weikersheim, tel. +49-(0)79 34/83 64. Open: Apr – Oct daily 9 a.m. – 6 p.m., Nov – Mar daily 10 a.m. – 12 p.m. & 1.30 – 4.30 p.m.)*
Weikersheim is also home to the **Tauberländer Dorfmuseum** which gives a detailed documentation of Franconian village life in the Tauber Valley.

10 Schweizer Stuben

The Schweizer Stuben hotel-restaurant complex near Wertheim combines no less than **three gourmet restaurants** under its roof: **Schober Landgasthof** serves Swiss specialities, while **Taverna La Vigna** treats its guests to the fine Italian cuisine that has won it a star from the Guide Michelin restaurant guide. **Schweizer Stuben** boast even two stars for their delicious dishes à la provençale.
(Bettingen, Geiselbrunnweg 11, tel. +49-(0)9342/30 70)

Wine Festivals

From April to October a number of traditional festivals celebrating local wines and *Federweißer* (new wine) invite to the lovely **Tauber Valley wine country.** The precise dates can be obtained from **Tourismusgemeinschaft Liebliches Taubertal.** *(Tauberbischofsheim, tel. +49-(0)93 41/8 22 94, fax -8 23 66)*

11 Bronnbach Cistercian Monastery

The monastery, founded in 1157, has a basilica with a nave and two side aisles, a well-preserved cloister and Late Romanesque chapterhouse, offering visitors excellent insight into the much-praised **architecture of the Cistercian order.**
(Bronnbach, tel. +49-(0)93 41/8 20. Open: Apr – Oct Mon – Sat 9.15 a.m. – 12 p.m. & 2 – 5 p.m., Sun 12.30 – 5 p.m.)

12 Further information

Tourismusgemeinschaft Liebliches Taubertal, Postfach 1254, D–97932 Tauberbischofsheim. Tel. +49-(0)9341/8 22 94, fax -8 23 66.
Kultur- und Fremdenverkehrsamt, Marktplatz 2, D–91541 Rothenburg ob der Tauber. Tel. +49-(0)9861/4 04 92, fax -8 68 07.

Promenade in style in the gardens of Schloss Weikersheim (left). The simple forms of the cloister at Bronnbach Cistercian Monastery still effuse the spirit of the Romanesque.

Fun and a great atmosphere are natural ingredients of any of the Tauber Valley's wine festivals.

1 **12**
The numbers 1 – 12 refer to positions marked on the map on pages 2 and 3.

CHRONOLOGICAL TABLE

C. 735 St. Boniface founds a nunnery in Bischofsheim.

C. 970 The Counts of Kochergau erect a castle in the Tauber Valley which forms the nucleus of Rothenburg.

1356 Rothenburg Castle is destroyed by an earthquake.

1383 – 1408 Rothenburg flourishes and builds up an impressive territory within the space of a few years.

Rothenburg's Burgtor is the only part of the castle to survive the earthquake of 1356 almost undamaged. There are many interesting details hidden away beneath the ivy. A ceiling fresco in the Josephssaal at Bronnbach Monastery (right) shows the complex in its original state.

1009 Henry II grants Wertheim market rights.

1142 After the last in the line of counts dies, Conrad III acquires Rothenburg Castle and methodically turns the castle settlement into a town.

1157 Cistercian monks from Maulbronn found a daughter monastery in Bronnbach.

1219 Brothers Henry, Andrew and Frederick of Hohenlohe give the Teutonic Order their lands in and around Mergentheim.

1274 King Rudolph of Hapsburg makes Rothenburg free city of the Holy Roman Empire.

1408 Heinrich Toppler, the most powerful mayor in Rothenburg's history, is executed in the dungeons under the town hall on June 13.

1476 Hans Böhm, the "piper of Niklashausen", proclaims "Heaven on Earth" in the Tauber Valley. The outspoken lay preacher is arrested on the orders of Würzburg's prince-bishop and burnt at the stake as a heretic.

From 1522/23 onwards The Reformation comes to Rothenburg ob der Tauber.

1525 Peasant War in the Tauber Valley.

1526 – 1806 The Grand and German Masters of the Teutonic Order reside in Bad Mergentheim.

1618 – 1648 During the Thirty Years' War Rothenburg is taken alternately by Royalist and Protestant troops.

1757 Almost completely unable to defend itself, Rothenburg ob der Tauber is attacked and plundered by 35 hussars under one Prussian lieutenant.

1802 Bavarian soldiers occupy Rothenburg. The town loses its rights as a free city.

1858 Carl Spitzweg paints in Rothenburg ob der Tauber.

1865 Wilhelm Heinrich Riehl's essay "A journey through the Tauber Valley is a journey through German history" sparks off tourist discovery of the Tauber Valley.

1881 Premiere of the *Meistertrunk* drama in Rothenburg.

1945 On Easter Saturday ca. 300 houses, 9 towers and 2,460 feet of Rothenburg's town wall fall victim to the ferocious attack of an American bomb squadron during the Second World War. The damage has more or less been compensated for with reconstructions erected since then.

1950 The Romantische Straße, Germany's first tourist route, comes into being.

1954 Emil Beck launches the Tauberbischofsheim sport club's fencing group.

1971 The first Reichsstadt Festtage take place in Rothenburg ob der Tauber to celebrate Rothenburg being made a free city 700 years ago.

The Kunigundenkapelle in Burgerroth fascinates with its mysterious sculptured decorations from the Romanesque period.

Rothenburg ob der Tauber will enter the next millennium under the protection of its mighty walls (below).

INDEX

Left:
Wertheim's Spitzer Turm has watched over the confluence of the Tauber and the Main for around 800 years.

ROTHENBURG
AND THE
TAUBER VALLEY

Detailed tourist tips on pages 64/65

1 Bad Mergentheim

2 Grafschaftsmuseum, Wertheim

3 Hotel-Restaurant Laurentius, Weikersheim

4 Käthe Wohlfahrts Weihnachtsdorf, Rothenburg

5 Kurmainzer Schloss, Tauberbischofsheim

6 Kriminalmuseum and Puppenmuseum, Rothenburg

7 Reichsstadtmuseum, Rothenburg

8 Tilman Riemenschneider's masterpieces

9 Schloss Weikersheim

10 Schweizer Stuben hotel-restaurant complex, Bettingen

11 Bronnbach Cistercian Monastery

Stürtz-REGIO.
Practical, packed with
illustrations – great souvenirs.
Stürtz Verlag GmbH,
Beethovenstraße 5,
D-97080 Würzburg